Dear Parent:
Your child's love of reading starts here!

Every child learns to read in a different way and at his or her own speed. Some go back and forth between reading levels and read favorite books again and again. Others read through each level in order. You can help your young reader improve and become more confident by encouraging his or her own interests and abilities. From books your child reads with you to the first books he or she reads alone, there are I Can Read Books for every stage of reading:

SHARED READING
Basic language, word repetition, and whimsical illustrations, ideal for sharing with your emergent reader

BEGINNING READING
Short sentences, familiar words, and simple concepts for children eager to read on their own

READING WITH HELP
Engaging stories, longer sentences, and language play for developing readers

READING ALONE
Complex plots, challenging vocabulary, and high-interest topics for the independent reader

I Can Read Books have introduced children to the joy of reading since 1957. Featuring award-winning authors and illustrators and a fabulous cast of beloved characters, I Can Read Books set the standard for beginning readers.

A lifetime of discovery begins with the magical words "I Can Read!"

Visit www.icanread.com for information
on enriching your child's reading experience.

For the Linebrook boys.
You light up my life!
—L.H.H.

I dedicate this book to my parents,
José María and Aurora.
—G.M.

I Can Read® and I Can Read Book® are trademarks of HarperCollins Publishers.

Thomas Edison: Lighting the Way
Copyright © 2019 by HarperCollins Publishers
All rights reserved. Manufactured in China. No part of this book may be used or reproduced in any manner whatsoever without written permission except in the case of brief quotations embodied in critical articles and reviews. For information address HarperCollins Children's Books, a division of HarperCollins Publishers, 195 Broadway, New York, NY 10007.
www.icanread.com

Library of Congress Control Number: 2019933062
ISBN 978-0-06-243288-9 (trade bdg.)—ISBN 978-0-06-243287-2 (pbk.)

Typography by Marisa Rother
20 21 22 23 SCP 10 9 8 7 6 5 4 3 2
❖   First Edition

THOMAS EDISON
Lighting the Way

by Lori Haskins Houran
pictures by Gustavo Mazali

HARPER
An Imprint of HarperCollinsPublishers

Thomas Edison is famous

for inventing the light bulb.

Only he DIDN'T invent it!

Not exactly.

Other inventors made light bulbs

before Edison was even born.

They figured out how to use

electricity to light them.

But there was a problem.

THE EDISON INCANDESCENT ELECTRIC LIGHT

The bulbs would start to glow.

Then—POOF!—they'd go out.

What good were those?

Edison wanted to invent
a light bulb that stayed lit.
Then people could use electricity
instead of oil lamps and candles
to light their homes.

Thomas Edison had been fascinated

by electricity since he was a boy.

When he was twelve,

he read about the telegraph.

It was a machine that used

electricity to send messages

along a wire.

Thomas built his own telegraph

and one for his friend James.

He strung wire between their houses.

Tap. Tap. Tap.

The telegraphs worked!

The boys could send each other

secret messages!

Thomas got to know

the telegraph operator

at the train station, Mr. Mackenzie.

One day, Thomas saw

Mr. Mackenzie's little boy

playing on the tracks.

A train was rolling right at him!

Thomas grabbed the boy just in time.

Mr. Mackenzie was grateful.

He helped Thomas become

a real telegraph operator.

Thomas liked the work.

He thought the telegraph

was a good machine,

but he wanted to improve it.

So Thomas found ways to make

the telegraph faster and better.

Thomas came up with ideas
for brand-new machines, too.
Companies were impressed.
They paid him for his ideas.
Thomas quit his job
and became a full-time inventor.

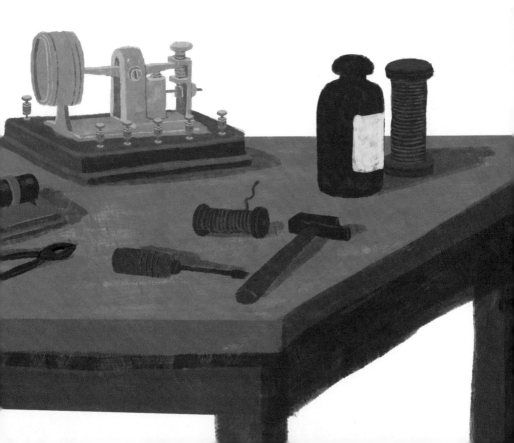

Thomas opened up a big lab
in Menlo Park, New Jersey.
It became known as
his "invention factory."

Thomas hired workers to build
the things he imagined.
One of his ideas was a machine
that could record sounds
and play them back.
No one had ever made one before.
Was it even possible?

Thomas drew sketches
of the machine.

His workers put it together.

"Mary had a little lamb,"
Thomas called into it.

He turned the handle.

Mary had a little lamb, he heard.

Thomas was shocked.

The machine worked on the first try!

The world was shocked, too.

What a magical invention!

People started calling Thomas

the Wizard of Menlo Park.

Soon the Wizard was ready for

his next challenge: the light bulb.

Thomas looked at the bulbs

other inventors had made.

He saw why they went out.

Their filaments burned up too fast.

A filament is the thin loop

inside a light bulb that glows

when electricity heats it.

Thomas began searching for

a new filament—one that would glow

for hours, not minutes.

Thomas looked for over a year.

He tried all sorts of things:

Fishing line. Grass.

Wire. Wood shavings.

Even bits of coconut shell.

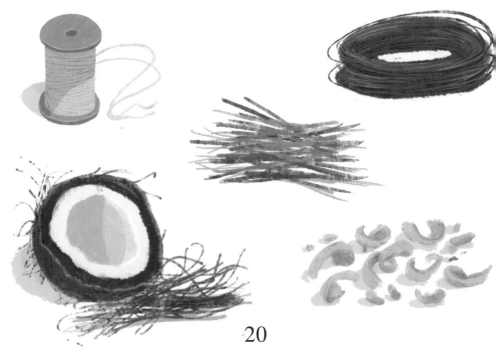

Finally, Thomas tried a piece
of thread, baked in an oven.
It worked!
Thomas's new light bulb glowed
for thirteen hours straight!

News spread of the breakthrough.

People rushed to Menlo Park

to see for themselves.

These lights didn't flicker
like candles or smoke like oil.
Instead, they glowed,
soft and steady and bright.
"Oooooh," gasped the crowd.
The Wizard had made magic again!

Thomas kept improving his bulbs.

He made one that lasted

over a thousand hours.

Now THAT was a useful light bulb!

Just as Thomas had hoped,
people began lighting
their homes with electricity.
Soon light bulbs took the place
of oil lamps and candles.
Today, more than two billion
light bulbs are made every year!

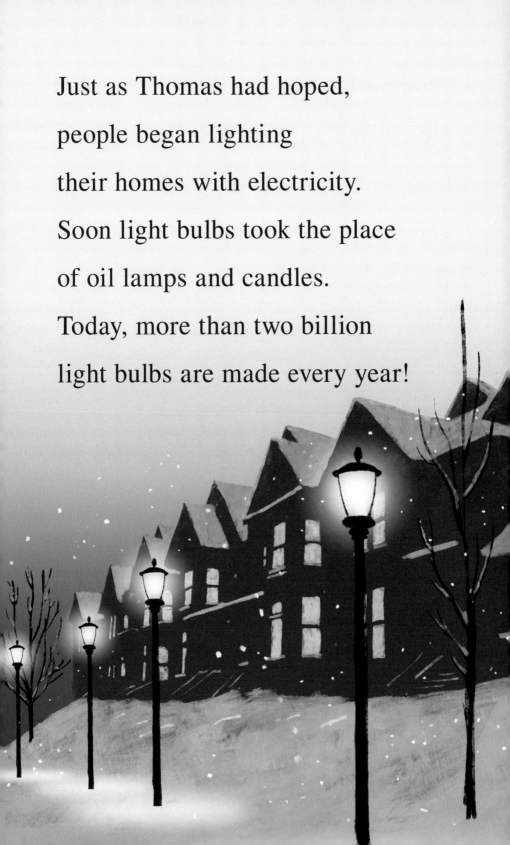

Thomas kept inventing his whole life.
He created a movie camera,
a copy machine, a car battery,
and many more things.
But it's his work on the light bulb
that people remember most.

Thomas died on October 18, 1931.
Three nights later, the president
asked Americans to turn off
their lights for one minute.
It was the perfect way to honor
the inventor who lit up our world.

Timeline

1847
Thomas Edison is
born on February 11.

1862
Starts working as a
telegraph operator

1876
Opens the "invention factory"
in Menlo Park, New Jersey

1877
Invents the phonograph,
the first machine to record
sounds and play them back

1879
Invents a useful,
reliable light bulb

1891
Invents the kinetograph,
an early movie camera

1893
Builds the world's first
movie studio in West
Orange, New Jersey

1896
Invents an X-ray viewer
called the fluoroscope

1901
Invents a battery for
electric cars

1931
Dies on October 18

1850
1860
1870
1880
1890
1900
1910
1920
1930

Edison had six children. He loved his family, but he spent more time in his lab than at home.

Edison fishing with one of his sons

Thomas Edison was hard of hearing from the time he was a boy. He said his deafness didn't hold him back. Instead, it helped him work. He could ignore all the noise around him!

Edison at age fourteen

Often he worked twenty-four hours at a time, stopping for quick naps.

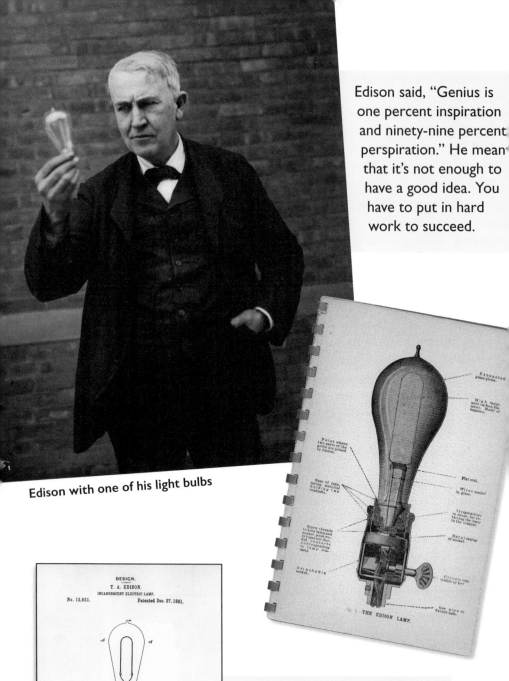

Edison said, "Genius is one percent inspiration and ninety-nine percent perspiration." He mean that it's not enough to have a good idea. You have to put in hard work to succeed.

Edison with one of his light bulbs

A patent is a paper from the government that shows you are the creator of an invention. Edison received 1,093 US patents in his lifetime.

A patent for the light bulb

Edison's favorite invention was his phonograph. He was invited to the White House in 1878 to demonstrate it for President Rutherford B. Hayes. The president was amazed. He woke up the First Lady in the middle of the night so she could hear it, too!

Edison with his favorite invention

Edison closed his first invention factory in 1882. The buildings began to fall apart. Some of them burned down. But in 1929, Edison's friend Henry Ford hired an architect to build a copy of the Menlo Park lab in Dearborn, Michigan. Today, visitors can go there and see just what the lab looked like when Edison worked on the light bulb.

Find Out More

To see the replica of the Menlo Park lab, visit Greenfield Village in Dearborn, Michigan *(https://www.thehenryford.org)*.

Visit the Thomas Edison Center at Menlo Park in Menlo Park, New Jersey *(http://www.menloparkmuseum.org)* and the Thomas Edison National Historical Park in West Orange, New Jersey *(www.nps.gov/edison)* to learn more about Edison and his work.